NAZI GERMANY

HISTORY IN AN HOUR

Also in the *History in an Hour* series

Nazi Germany

History in an Hour

RUPERT COLLEY

WILLIAM
COLLINS

William Collins
An imprint of HarperCollins*Publishers* Ltd
77–85 Fulham Palace Road
Hammersmith, London W6 8JB
www.harpercollins.co.uk

Visit the History in an Hour website:
www.historyinanhour.com

Published by William Collins in 2013

First published as an eBook by Harper*Press* in 2011

1

A catalogue record for this book
is available from the British Library

ISBN 978-0-00-753914-7

Find out more about HarperCollins and the environment at
www.harpercollins.co.uk/green

Contents

Introduction

'And so it had all come to this. Did all this happen only so that a gang of wretched criminals could lay hands on the fatherland? Hatred grew in me, hatred for those responsible for this deed.' The words are those of Adolf Hitler: the deed is Germany's surrender in the First World War; the wretched criminals are the politicians who had meekly accepted the surrender and the defeat of Germany after the First World War.

Fifteen years later, Hitler was appointed chancellor of Germany and the Third Reich had been born. Destined, Hitler predicted, to last a thousand years, Hitler's Nazi Germany lasted a mere twelve. Yet, within those few years, Hitler's regime wrought devastation, total war and mass genocide.

How did Hitler rise to power, and how did the Nazi Party eliminate all opponents? How did he exploit the use of state control and propaganda? What was life like in Nazi Germany for women, families and Jews? How did Hitler manipulate foreign policy to achieve his aims and bring about war? This, in an hour, is Nazi Germany.

The German Revolution:
The End of the Second Reich

In October 1918, sailors at the port of Kiel disobeyed orders to fight the British fleet. It was, as they saw it, a pointless and suicidal mission. The revolt soon spread throughout Germany. The province of Bavaria went so far as to establish a socialist republic along Soviet lines. The Kaiser, Wilhelm II, the unhinged grandson of Queen Victoria, abdicated on 9 November 1918, two days before the armistice, and the chancellor, Prince Max of Baden, appointed a left-wing coalition government and handed over the chancellorship to Friedrich Ebert.

With the abdication of the Kaiser and the collapse of Imperial Germany (the Second Reich – or empire), Ebert proclaimed Germany a republic, formed a provisional government (a temporary arrangement until elections could be held) and, on 11 November 1918, signed the armistice that brought the Great War to an end.

But the social unrest continued. In January 1919 the German

Communist Party, the Spartacists, staged an uprising in Berlin. Rosa Luxemburg, leader of the movement, had opposed the uprising, arguing that the time was not yet right for communism. But she was unable to contain the fury of the left and Chancellor Ebert turned to the right-wing Freikorps, or Free Corps, for assistance. After three days of intense street fighting the Freikorps, a band of demobilized, nationalistic soldiers, had, with extreme violence, crushed the rebellion. Luxemburg was arrested and killed while in police custody.

The Weimar Republic: A Republic Is Born

The first German democratic election took place the same month, January 1919, attracting an 83 per cent turnout and resulting in the formation of a National Constituent Assembly. The situation in Berlin was still volatile so on 6 February the Assembly met for the first time in the town of Weimar and there drew up a new constitution. Six months later the constitution was ratified and the Weimar Republic was born. However, disturbances continued, especially in Berlin and Bavaria, and Ebert again had to call in the Freikorps to keep order. In March 1919 the Freikorps went to work and the Socialist Republic in Bavaria was brought to a bloody end.

The Treaty of Versailles:
'An armistice for twenty years'

On 28 June 1919, Germany reluctantly signed the Paris Peace Settlement in the Hall of Mirrors at the Palace of Versailles – exactly five years on from the assassination of Archduke Franz Ferdinand, the spark that had ignited the First World War. Germany had not been permitted to take part in the talks and was too weak, politically and militarily, to resist the terms dictated by the representatives of thirty-two nations, led by the Allied powers – the US, Britain, France and Italy.

The terms were harsh and not for negotiation. Germany lost 13 per cent of her territory, which meant 12 per cent of Germans now lived in a foreign country, and Germany's colonial possessions were redistributed among the other colonial powers. The German Rhineland, on the border with France, was to be demilitarized (stripped of an armed presence) and placed under Allied control until 1935. The small but industrially important Saar region was to be governed by Britain and France for fifteen years, and its coal exported to France in recompense for the French coal mines destroyed by Germany during the war. After fifteen years a plebiscite (or referendum) of the Saar population would decide its future.

Most of West Prussia was given to Poland. The German city of Danzig (modern-day Gdansk) was made a 'free' city so that Poland could have use of a port not situated in Germany. To give Poland access to Danzig, they were given a strip of land, the 'Polish Corridor', through Prussia, thereby cutting East Prussia off from the rest of Germany.

Militarily, Germany's army was to be limited to a token 100,000 men, and its navy to 15,000, plus a ban on conscription. She was not permitted to have an air force, nor tanks, and was prohibited from producing or importing weaponry.

The payment of reparations was for 'compensation for all damage done to the civilian population of the Allied powers and their property'. It was to include raw material, such as the coal from the Saar and Ruhr regions. Two years later, in 1921, the cost of reparations was announced – £6.6 billion, which German economists calculated would take until 1988 to pay. The figure shocked and angered Germans who conveniently forgot that Germany had demanded an even greater sum from a defeated France following the Franco-Prussian War of 1870–71.

But it was the humiliating clause that forced Germany into accepting responsibility for the war and for the damage to the civilian populations of the Allies that rankled most with the public at home.

The treaty satisfied no one. Germany was outraged. Britain thought it too harsh, believing an economically weak Germany would be detrimental to all Europe; the US, also considering it harsh, refused to ratify the treaty or to join the newly formed

League of Nations; and the French felt it not harsh enough. It was they, the French argued, who had suffered most during the war. The French public were so dissatisfied with their president, Clemenceau, that they voted him out six months later, replacing him with Ferdinand Foch who, with sharp intuition, said, 'This is not peace, this is an armistice for twenty years.'

The Weimar government, although democratically elected, was deemed responsible for Germany's humiliation, and criticized by all sides for its weakness in standing up to the Allies. In March 1920 the Freikorps, led by Wolfgang Kapp, tried to seize power in Berlin but the coup, unable to gain the army's support, failed.

DAP: Member 555

The Kapp Putsch, as it became known, may have failed but it illustrated the feeling of anger among the extreme right in Germany. Among the many small political parties was the German Workers' Party or, to use its German abbreviation, DAP, set up in 1919 by 35-year-old Munich locksmith, Anton Drexler. The DAP, a far-right party that aimed to appeal to the workers, consisted of only about fifty members but, to give the impression of greater numbers, began their membership cards at number five hundred.

It was to a meeting of this party in September 1919 that Adolf Hitler, at this stage being groomed by the army as a political instructor, was sent to observe and speak. The beer hall meeting consisted of only about twenty attendees but Hitler's speech so impressed Drexler that he was invited to join the party. With membership number 555 (although he later claimed in *Mein*

Kampf that he was the seventh member), he signed his name as 'Hittler'.

NSDAP: Nationalism and Socialism under One Roof

Hitler's oratory and leadership skills were evident and he soon took over from Drexler as the DAP's leader. On 24 February 1920, still maintaining its peculiar mix of right-wing extremism and socialist ideals, the party lengthened its name to the Nationalist Socialist German Workers' Party, or NSDAP. Now boasting 3,000 members, the Nazi Party was born. Two months later Hitler resigned from the army to concentrate full time on expanding his party.

Corporal Hitler

Born in 1889 in Austria, Hitler spent much of his youth in Vienna, living in cheap accommodation, frequenting coffee houses and trying to sell his paintings. Art was his passion and his failure to secure a place at art school plunged him into depression. Resentment of the Jew was rife in the city and Hitler absorbed this anti-Semitism and, like many of his contemporaries, believed the Jew to be set apart from 'the rest of humanity', as he described in *Mein Kampf*.

At the outbreak of the First World War Hitler was in Munich and, having managed to avoid conscription into the Austrian army, signed up to a Bavarian regiment within the German army. He served as a messenger and did so with distinction throughout the war. Having no aspirations for promotion, he finished the war as a corporal, having twice been awarded the Iron Cross and twice wounded – the second time in October 1918 when he was temporarily blinded by mustard gas.

It was during his recuperation that the armistice was signed, leaving Hitler and many other Germans embittered. Germany had won the war in the east, and following the 'Spring Offensive' of 1918, looked well placed to win it in the west. But a strike of German munitions workers towards the end of the war, believed to have been organized by Jews, disrupted the supply of arms and the front-line soldier suffered as a consequence. The government had accepted defeat and most Germans felt it was they, the government, who had lost Germany the war. The signing seven months later of the Treaty of Versailles confirmed this sense of betrayal, the feeling that the German people had been 'stabbed in the back'.

As the new leader of the fledging Nazi Party, Hitler met Hermann Göring and Rudolf Hess, two men who would serve him well over the next twenty years, and Ernst Röhm, a tough ex-soldier and former member of the Freikorps, who went on to form the Nazi storm troopers (or SA).

The Nazi Manifesto: A Thousand Years

In February 1920 the party drew up its manifesto which, among its twenty-five points, demanded the union of all Germans into a greater Germany, and called for an expansion of living space to accommodate the growth of the German people. This space, *Lebensraum*, was to be found in the east at the expense of the Slavic races, who would, according to the party, be simply evicted.

The manifesto rejected the Treaty of Versailles – Germany needed to find her pride again and to rid the nation of the traitors who had so meekly accepted the peace of 1919. Hitler would lead such a Germany, a Third Reich that would reign for a thousand years.

The Jew, the source of German humiliation, was not and could not, stated the manifesto, be German. The manifesto maintained within its nationalist and anti-Semitic principles ones that were socialist in nature, designed to broaden its appeal to the German workers.

Nazism relied on the use of symbols – the swastika, which although far from new, was already identified with the Nazis, and, fifteen years later, in September 1935, was officially adopted as the national flag of Germany alongside a black, red and white tricolour. In *Mein Kampf* Hitler wrote about the colours of the flag: 'In the red we see the social idea of the movement; in the white, the nationalist idea and in the swastika the vision of the struggle for the victory of the Aryan man.'

Munich Putsch:
'The national revolution has begun'

Such was Hitler's hatred of the Weimar government that he decided
to overthrow it. On the evening of 8 November 1923, he led a
group of 600 storm troopers and together they burst into a Munich
beer hall meeting. The 34-year-old Hitler fired two shots from his
revolver into the ceiling, declaring that he was the new leader of
the German government and that the 'national revolution has
begun'.

Meanwhile, Röhm had seized the city's war ministry. Hitler had
expected the support of the army and the Bavarian police and
then to march on to Berlin. But the support never materialized
and the following day, as Hitler led 300 Nazis through the streets
of Munich to meet Röhm, the police blocked their way. The Nazis
refused to stop and the police opened fire, killing sixteen and
wounding many more. Hitler hurled himself to the ground, dislo-
cating his shoulder, then tried to make a run for it, but was caught

and arrested. It was later claimed he was trying to get a wounded child to hospital. The Munich Putsch may have failed but Hitler learnt a useful lesson – that power could not be secured through force but would have to be earned through legitimate means and the ballot box.

Mein Kampf:
'Lies, Stupidity and Cowardice'

Hitler was tried for high treason and could have faced the death penalty but got away with a lenient sentence of five years. He served less than nine months. Although frequently depressed and talking of suicide, Hitler used his time in prison constructively, dictating to Hess his autobiographical, ideological rant, *Mein Kampf*. Published in two volumes, the first on 18 July 1925, the second in 1926, it was originally entitled *My 4½ Year Struggle Against Lies, Stupidity and Cowardice*, the new title being suggested by his publisher.

Much of it is devoted to race; the need for a pure race of German Aryans, untainted by the blood of different races. The Aryan race was of the highest order, the 'bearers of culture'; the Jewish race (Hitler defined Jews by race not religion) of the lowest. The aim was to eliminate the Jews (referred to throughout the book by various unpleasant metaphors: parasites, germs, vermin) from society. He expanded on many of the themes of the Nazi manifesto, including *Lebensraum*, the union of all German-speaking people and the treachery of the Treaty of Versailles. *Mein Kampf* sold poorly at first and a second book, written in 1928, was never published. However, by 1939 it was outselling all other titles in Germany with the exception of the Bible.

The Ruhr: An Economic Downturn

The Weimar government was struggling to pay the reparations demanded by the Treaty of Versailles. The views of the Allied powers differed: the US had taken the isolationist route and paid little attention to what was happening in Europe; while Italy was in the midst of a fascist takeover. Britain felt that Versailles had been too harsh and sought reconciliation with the Germans, and advocated a reduction in reparations to aid the recovery of the German economy, which, in turn, would benefit the economy of Europe as a whole. Only the French were determined that Germany should fully meet her obligations.

In 1923 the Ruhr industrialists had stopped supplying France with the requisite quota of German coal. The French and Belgian governments, angered by this breaking of the rules, sent troops into the region. When the German workers of the Ruhr, affronted by this occupation, refused to work for the French, the French government sent in its own workforce. The occupation of the Ruhr caused chaos for Germany's economy, triggering a period of high unemployment and hyperinflation. The inflation wiped life savings out overnight: in 1921 the mark was worth one dollar. Two years later it was an unimaginable 4,000,000,000,000 to the dollar.

America began to realize, as had the British, that an economically unstable Germany would be detrimental to all Europe and tasked Charles Dawes, an American banker, to formulate a recovery programme. The Dawes Plan had the desired effect and from 1924 Germany enjoyed a period of relative prosperity. American loans and investment brought inflation down to a manageable level and unemployment fell. With American money, Germany began paying the French, Belgian and British reparations, albeit at a lesser rate, and the Allied nations, in turn, were able to start repaying their war debts to the US. It was an unending circular movement of money. By 1925 the French and Belgians had withdrawn from the Ruhr.

On the international stage, too, relations between Germany and its European neighbours became less tense, ending Germany's sense of isolation, and leading, in 1926, to Germany joining the League of Nations. In 1929, based on the recommendation of the American-commissioned Young Plan (after its author Owen D. Young), reparations were cut by 75 per cent. Following the Great Depression payments were suspended for a year and by 1931 reparations were dropped altogether. Germany had paid back only an eighth of the original demand.

Following the failed Munich Putsch, Hitler's name had become known throughout Germany. However, during the Weimar years of relative economic stability the Nazis were marginalized and, even on Hitler's release, lacked electoral support, rarely polling more than 3 per cent throughout the 1920s.

The Great Depression: The Crash

It was the knock-on effect of America's Great Depression that changed the political landscape in Germany. Following the Wall Street Crash of October 1929 America called in its worldwide loans on which Germany, especially, was overly reliant. The stable years had come to an abrupt halt.

Unemployment soared – in one month alone, January 1930, unemployment rose from 1.5 million to 2.5 million; by 1931, 4 million were unemployed; and by 1933, 6 million. The Weimar government, in an attempt to keep things under control, adopted a policy of deflation, causing severe wage cuts and further unemployment. Businesses went bankrupt, banks collapsed.

The Weimar government had failed its people. The country was in economic ruin, people's livelihoods were shattered, and the nation, still burdened with the humiliation of Versailles, was fearful of the communists and the Jews. They looked for an alternative and that alternative lay in Adolf Hitler and the Nazi Party.

As unemployment rocketed so did the number of Nazi Party members, rising from about 120,000 members in mid-1929 to over a million within a year. This was reflected in the elections – from 2.5 per cent of the vote in May 1928 to over 18 per cent in September 1930.

Nazi Elections: 'He can lick stamps with my head on them'

However, it was 1932 that saw the rise of the Nazi Party into a prominent political force. In the July 1932 Reichstag elections the Nazi Party polled almost 40 per cent of the vote, making it the most powerful party. There was a slight dip in the elections four months later but the party still had enough electoral clout that Hitler, as dictated by the Weimar constitution, should have been appointed chancellor. But the Weimar president, the 84-year-old Paul von Hindenburg, was reluctant to appoint the former corporal: 'That man a chancellor?' he said. 'I'll make him a post-master and he can lick stamps with my head on them.'

Following the November elections, Hindenburg replaced von Papen as chancellor with Kurt von Schleicher (whom, two years later, Hitler had murdered during the 'Night of the Long Knives'). While von Schleicher tried to form a coalition, von Papen decided he could work with Hitler. In a power-sharing partnership, Hitler would become chancellor and von Papen would serve as his vice-chancellor. But von Papen would hold the real power, as he persuaded the ageing president. Hitler, von Papen argued, needed to be contained and this would be far easier with Hitler working inside the government than agitating from outside. 'In two months,' said von Papen, 'we'll have pushed Hitler into a corner where he can squeal to his heart's content.'

Reluctantly, Hindenburg agreed. And so on 30 January 1933, Hitler was appointed chancellor within a coalition government. He had done it: Hitler had achieved what he had striven for since 1923 – power through legitimate means. That evening, 30 January, Hitler looked out from his balcony at the Chancellery. Beneath him thousands of torch-bearing Nazis filed past. This was their moment of triumph, the day of national exultation; the Nazi era had begun and their mood was jubilant.

Von Papen was soon to realize the folly of his intrigue – it was he, not Hitler, who was pushed into a corner and who would become an inconsequential figure. Barely a month after Hitler's appointment came the Reichstag Fire, started, whether accidentally or not, by 24-year-old Marinus van der Lubbe, a Dutch arsonist who may or may not have been a communist. Rumours persisted that it was the Nazis themselves that set the parliament building ablaze.

Either way, Hitler saw it as a 'God-given signal' and made political capital out of it, blaming the communists, having all political opponents rounded up and beaten and put into 'protective custody'. Hindenburg, increasingly senile, accepted Hitler's request following the fire for a decree suspending all political and civil liberties as a 'temporary' measure for the 'protection of the people and state'. These temporary measures were never revoked. A year later van der Lubbe was executed.

In March the last parliamentary elections took place. Only Hitler, it was claimed, could save Germany from the communists, and the SA, using violence and intimidation, silenced all other parties. The Nazis polled 44 per cent of the vote, not enough for a majority but enough to quash any future political resistance.

Enabling Act: 'Fanatics, hooligans and eccentrics have got the upper hand'

The post of chancellor was one that lasted for four years before another election. But Hitler requested more than the prescribed amount of time to deal with the nation's problems. He proposed the Enabling Act in order to allow him greater time and to dispense with the constitution and the electoral system. Constitutionally, Hitler needed a two-thirds majority to pass the act. Having bullied and threatened any potential opposition into silence, the Reichstag convened in the Berlin Opera House, its grand hall lined with storm troopers. Only the Socialist Democrats were brave enough to vote against the proposal but the act was easily passed by 441 votes to 84. There would be neither more elections nor a constitution to keep Hitler in check. The Reichstag had, in effect, voted away its power.

Within a matter of weeks it had become illegal to criticize the government. A new secret police force was established, the Gestapo, which immediately began arresting 'unreliable' persons. They were accommodated in Dachau, the first concentration camp, opened near Munich within weeks of the Nazis coming to power. Trade unions were banned, freedom of the press curtailed, and all other political parties declared illegal, leaving only the Nazi Party. Germany had become a one-party state with Hitler its dictator.

The British ambassador to Germany watched these developments with increasing alarm and, having seen Hitler rip up the constitution, wrote: 'We are living in a country [Germany] where fanatics, hooligans and eccentrics have got the upper hand.'

The First Anti-Jew Laws: 'Non-citizens'

With the Enabling Act of March 1933 in place, the first of over 400 anti-Jewish measures were introduced. Now classed as 'Non-Aryans', the Jews were banned from teaching, receiving a university education, working in the civil service, media and the military and from owning businesses. Books by Jewish authors were banned, including works by Karl Marx and Sigmund Freud. The Jewish population suffered daily torment and anti-Semitic hysteria triggered a mass exodus of Jews from Germany. Of the half-million Jews in Germany in 1933, about 280,000 had emigrated by 1939, among them Albert Einstein and Marlene Dietrich. Many emigrated to the US but others chose eastern Europe where, once the war had broken out, they were soon caught in the Nazi war machine.

In September 1935, the same month as the swastika became the official flag of Germany, the Nuremberg Race Laws came into effect, legitimizing anti-Semitism as part of the Nazi state. Deemed as 'non-citizens', Jews were denied German citizenship and all political and civil rights. The laws drew up definitions of Jewishness (depending on parents and grandparents), and prohibited marriage between Jews and Germans. Despite his rabid hatred of Jews, Hitler was, at this stage, still a relative moderate in how far to push state-sponsored anti-Semitism, resisting calls from within his party for more radical measures. Of the four drafts of the Nuremberg Laws presented to him, Hitler chose the most moderate. His moderation was motivated purely by diplomatic concerns, not wanting to overly outrage international opinion. He ordered, for example, a temporary suspension of media-led anti-Semitism during the Berlin Olympics of 1936.

Night of the Long Knives: 'The Führer's soldierly decision and exemplary courage'

Hitler's power was now almost absolute. But the excesses of the SA were troubling him. Their violence, which once, as a revolutionary, Hitler would have endorsed, had become an embarrassment. Having gained power Hitler wanted to win over the German people and international opinion through legitimate means, not by force. Still led by Röhm, the SA felt that Hitler was going soft and had not given them their due reward for helping the Nazis into power. They started talking of a 'second revolution' with Röhm as the leader of a People's Party, which greatly alarmed the industrialists and businessmen that Hitler had managed to woo. Röhm wanted also to merge the army with the SA under his command, which, in turn, alarmed the army and its chief, Werner von Blomberg.

In April 1934, Hitler and Blomberg signed a secret pact. Hitler promised Blomberg and the army full control of the military (ahead of Röhm's SA), and, in return, Blomberg told Hitler that he could rely on the army's support when the time came for Hitler to claim the presidency following the anticipated death of the 86-year-old Hindenburg. Himmler, as head of the SS (a similar but rival group to the SA), and Göring also feared Röhm. Between them, they concocted false evidence that Röhm was planning a coup against Hitler. The SA's agitation was beginning to jeopardize the country's stability, and Hindenburg threatened to impose martial law unless Hitler could bring the situation under control. In other words – deal with Röhm and the SA.

On the weekend of 30 June–1 July 1934, in what was to become known as the 'Night of the Long Knives', Hitler acted. Members of the SS stormed a hotel in the village of Bad Wiessee where the SA had gathered for a weekend of homosexual debauchery, pulled Röhm and his henchmen from their beds and had them arrested. They were all promptly executed, including Röhm who, having passed up the opportunity to take his own life, was shot.

Hitler used the purge to rid himself of anyone whom he disliked or who had crossed him in the past, including the last chancellor of the Weimar Republic, Kurt von Schleicher. The 'Night of the Long Knives' claimed over 200 lives. Hindenburg congratulated his chancellor for having acted so swiftly. The army, having seen its rival demolished, sided with Hitler, and Blomberg applauded the 'Führer's soldierly decision and exemplary courage'.

The Führer: 99 Per Cent Approval

A month later, on 2 August 1934, the 86-year-old president died. The night before, Hitler visited him and the old man, now senile and mistaking Hitler for the old kaiser, called him 'Your Majesty'. Immediately after Hindenburg's death Hitler took the opportunity to combine the posts of chancellor and president, adopting the title Führer, and, as president, inherited the post of supreme commander of the armed forces. Blomberg ordered that the armed forces swear an oath of personal allegiance to Hitler himself, rather than to the president or state. In a referendum on 19 August over 90 per cent of Germans approved of Hitler's absolute power and the merging of the two most important posts. In a mockery of an election the following year, in which the Nazis were the only party allowed to stand, Hitler won 99 per cent approval.

Nazi Party membership rocketed. By 1939, 25 per cent of the adult population were members. But the pre-1933 members regarded the more recent ones with disdain, suspecting that their joining was less to do with conviction than expediency and self-advancement.

Nazi Germany and the Economy: 'Guns will make us strong; butter will make us fat'

At the point Hitler came to power, Germany's economy had begun to improve following the chaos of the Great Depression. Hitler took full credit. Gearing the economy for war, Hitler did not want Germany to be dependent on imports, and his first economics minister, Hjalmar Schacht, advanced Hitler's objective of trying to secure autarky (economic self-sufficiency). Schacht also introduced public work schemes, such as the building of motorways, schools and hospitals, thereby greatly reducing unemployment, which fell from 6 million in 1933 to 1 million in 1938.

But Schacht began questioning Hitler's war economy, believing it to be too costly for the country to cope with. However, Hitler believed that Germany's expansion to the east and the eviction of the indigenous Slavic population would cause conflict with Britain and France. The economy, therefore, needed to be ready for war within four years. Schacht's recommendations of a slowdown did not fit in with Hitler's plans, so in 1936 Hitler replaced him with Göring. In 1944 Schacht was implicated in the July Bomb Plot on Hitler's life. However, he managed to avoid execution and, having spent time in a concentration camp, survived the war.

Göring's grasp of economics was questionable but, with Hitler's prompting, he introduced the Four-Year Plan, a more aggressive policy for achieving autarky. The economy continued to improve, but it was less to do with economic efficiency and more to do with rapid rearmament: 'Guns will make us strong; butter will make us fat,' said Göring, a fine example of one who had overindulged in butter. By the time war came in 1939 Germany was still heavily reliant on the import of foodstuffs and raw materials. Autarky was never achieved.

State Control: Guilty Before Innocent

The state secret police, the Gestapo, and Heinrich Himmler's SS kept the population under control. Following Dachau, more concentration camps were built where enemies of the people (criminals, homosexuals, gypsies, beggars, Jews, communists and anyone out of step with the regime) were placed for 'protective custody'. For the average German it was seen as a time of security as crime fell drastically, and many were happy to play the role of informant, which helped the Gestapo and the SS keep the camps full. With the loss of civil liberty, those put on trial were assumed guilty and stood little chance of acquittal.

State Control: Guilty Before Innocent

The Family:
'I detest women who dabble in politics'

The family was central to Nazi ideology – people were encouraged to get married and have children. Honeymooning couples were given a copy of *Mein Kampf* to savour. Abortion was made illegal and the purchase of contraceptives frowned upon. Financial incentives to have children were given to parents in the form of loans where the interest rate fell with each new child. By the fourth child the interest would be cancelled out.

Each year, on 12 August (the birthday of Hitler's mother), the Motherhood Cross was awarded to mothers of large families: a Motherhood Iron Cross for mothers of four children, up a sliding scale culminating in the Cross of Gold and Diamond for those with ten children. For these finest examples of motherhood, Hitler acted as honorary godfather. Hitler Youth boys were expected to salute bearers of the cross. The mother was a heroine: 'I have donated a child to the Führer,' read one famous poster. The mother, according to Hitler, held the same rank of honour in society as the soldier.

Women were told not to work and they were certainly not allowed to be part of the Nazi hierarchy: 'I detest women who dabble in politics,' said Hitler; 'in no local section of the party has a woman ever had the right to hold even the smallest post.' The woman's place was very much in the home. Women were encouraged to join the various Nazi leagues – the National Socialist Womanhood being one – while girls joined the female equivalent of the Hitler Youth, the League of German Maidens.

By 1939 almost 90 per cent of boys were members of the Hitler Youth. With slogans like 'We are born to die for Germany', the boys attended frequent classes and summer camps where physical activity and outdoor skills went hand in hand with Nazi indoctrination.

For the 'handicapped', either mentally or physically, the Law for the Prevention of Progeny with Hereditary Diseases (1933) meant compulsory sterilization. By 1937 almost 200,000 adults or 'useless mouths' had been sterilized.

Propaganda: 'Where they burn books, they will also ultimately burn people'

Joseph Goebbels, as Hitler's minister for propaganda, controlled all forms of media. Independent newspapers were closed down. Only official Nazi newspapers, the control of which was carefully overseen by Goebbels and his ministry, were allowed to be printed. The production of radios greatly increased, providing further avenues of employment and allowing the party the means of extending its propaganda message. The Reich Radio Company, set up purely for propaganda purposes, gave Hitler the platform to deliver his frequent messages to the nation.

The cinema was also a favoured means of communication. Director Leni Riefenstahl made epic films, such as *Triumph des Willens* (The Triumph of the Will) and *Olympia*, which showed the Nazi Party in all its grandiose pomposity. Goebbels organized the huge Nuremberg rallies at which Hitler, the gifted orator, poured forth his message in increasingly hysterical rhetoric.

All art had to correspond to the party line, figurative depictions of the Nazi paradise or legends of German history being two favourite themes. Reflecting Hitler's personal tastes, modern or abstract art was considered degenerate. Artists, forced into conformity, produced work lacking creativity or spontaneity.

The works of over 20,000 writers were banned; their books were ceremoniously burnt on Berlin's Opernplatz in May 1933, including those of the nineteenth-century romantic poet and playwright, Heinrich Heine, whose famous line: 'Where they burn books, they will also ultimately burn people' is today engraved on a plaque at the site. The music of many great Jewish composers, Mahler, Mendelssohn, Schoenberg and others, fell out of favour.

The Olympics

The Berlin Olympics of 1936 gave Hitler the opportunity to show Nazism off to the world. The specially made 110,000-seater athletic stadium was filled to capacity throughout the games, attracting a total of 4 million visitors, including Hitler who attended each day. Richard Strauss composed the music for the opening ceremony. Hitler ordered a suspension of displays of anti-Semitism, not wanting to show Germany in a negative light, so the Jews were temporarily spared the daily vitriol of abuse. Jesse Owens of the US famously won four gold medals (including the 100 and 200 metres), prompting Hitler to enquire why there were so many black athletes on the American team. Germany, however, much to the Führer's satisfaction, finished the Games topping the medal table.

Kristallnacht: The Night of Broken Glass

The life of the German Jew became increasingly unbearable. Often assaulted and humiliated, their beards hacked off in public, made to do the dirtiest jobs, Jews were banned from more and more of German life. Prohibited from frequenting cafés, theatres, swimming pools and parks, Jews were driven out of towns that strove to be *Judenfrei*, Jew-free. Professional Jews were banned from practising, whether as lawyers, doctors or dentists.

The culmination of this offensive took place on the night of 9 November 1938, and was known as Kristallnacht or the Night of Broken Glass. Goebbels, using the pretext that a Jew had killed a German embassy official in Paris, initiated the pogrom, endorsed from above and enthusiastically carried out throughout the country. Jewish homes, synagogues and schools were burnt down; businesses looted and ransacked; thousands of Jews beaten up and nearly a hundred murdered. Twenty thousand Jews were arrested and deported to concentration camps and a 1-billion-Reichsmark fine imposed on the Jewish community to pay for the damage. International opinion was outraged but by now Hitler was confident enough to pay little attention to their protests.

More legislation was passed, prohibiting Jewish children from attending state schools and imposing strict curfews on movement. Speaking to the Reichstag in January 1939, Hitler was still referring back to the Jewish conspiracy that had supposedly defeated Germany at the end of the First World War: 'This day will be avenged,' he said, adding that another world war would result in the 'annihilation of the Jewish race in Europe'.

Foreign Policy: 'Germany will of its own accord never break the peace'

After coming to power, Hitler immediately set about ripping apart the Treaty of Versailles. The payment of reparations may have been quietly dropped, but the rest of the treaty remained in place. Four days after being appointed chancellor, Hitler spoke of the need for an expanded military force by 1938 so that Germany would be strong enough to make good his objective of finding living space in eastern Europe. But during these early years of power, Hitler usually hid his real intentions, claiming that Germany only wanted parity with the other European powers. Beyond these 'reasonable' demands, further military claims were not on the agenda: 'Germany will of its own accord never break the peace,' Hitler told one British correspondent in 1935.

Britain and Italy were prepared to discuss what they felt were legitimate claims but the French were unwilling to allow Germany permission to re-arm. This lack of compromise gave Hitler the excuse, in October 1933, to withdraw from both disarmament talks and the League of Nations. He talked insincerely of coming back to the League once it had addressed Germany's grievances but now, free of the League's interference, Hitler was able to step up Germany's rearmament programme.

In January 1934 Hitler signed a ten-year non-aggression pact with Poland. The Nazi Party bore a grudge against Poland, given the amount of German territory that was now part of this newly established country, so many in the Nazi Party questioned Hitler's motives for signing such a pact. But Hitler, in a clever and duplicitous piece of diplomatic manoeuvring, wanted to create the impression of a Germany accepting of the terms of the Treaty of Versailles and bearing no ill-feeling towards Poland.

In 1935 Hitler announced the existence of the German air force, the Luftwaffe, which had been built up in secret in direct violation of the Treaty of Versailles. He introduced conscription in another direct snub to the Allied powers and continued apace with rearmament. Britain, France and Italy were now sufficiently worried to meet in the Italian town of Stresa and form the Stresa Front to formally protest, as did the League of Nations, at Germany's blatant breaches of the treaty.

Hitler ignored such protests. France signed treaties with the Soviet Union and Czechoslovakia, which displeased the British, who in turn signed a naval agreement with Germany. The agreement allowed Germany to build a fleet of ships 35 per cent the size of Britain's, and with an equal number of submarines. Britain had, as France saw it, condoned Germany's total disregard for the Treaty of Versailles. The Stresa Front, now greatly weakened, collapsed entirely when, in October 1935, Italy invaded Abyssinia. Benito Mussolini, Italy's fascist leader since 1922, had been desperate for a show of military strength and the prestige of colonial conquest. Abyssinia was a member of the League of

Nations, and Britain and France, as leading lights of the League, should have protested, but fearful that in doing so they might push Mussolini on to Hitler's side, they decided to allow Italy its colonial triumph.

The Rhineland: 'We have no territorial claims to make in Europe'

The evident weakness of the League and the distraction caused by Mussolini's misadventures in Abyssinia encouraged Hitler to take his next step, another bold move against the terms of Versailles, when, in March 1936, he ordered his troops into the Rhineland. The use of the Rhineland as a military base had been banned as part of the treaty in order to protect France's eastern border against future German expansion.

Hitler's generals had tried to argue against such a manoeuvre, believing that it would force France's hand into retaliation. Hitler, however, was prepared to take the gamble. He sent only a modest number of troops and gave orders that if the French were to take up arms, they were to withdraw immediately. Had it been the case, Hitler's position may have looked vulnerable. But although the French protested they did nothing, and nor did the League. Economic sanctions against Germany, although an option, would have had an effect throughout Europe not just in Germany.

So, Hitler's gamble paid off, and his prestige at home, already high, was enhanced yet further. Italy, still in the midst of fighting against the Abyssinians, took no interest in events. Britain, feeling that Germany was merely reclaiming her own 'back garden', also did nothing. 'We have no territorial claims to make in Europe,' remarked Hitler as his troops marched into the Rhineland. Although violating Versailles, his claim was not untrue; after all, the area was part of Germany; Hitler had not invaded a foreign country.

Previously, the people of the Saar region had wanted a return to Germany. The Saar had been under the authority of the League of Nations since 1920 as part of the Treaty of Versailles, and its coal transported to France as part of the reparations package. Versailles had allowed for a plebiscite (or a referendum) after fifteen years, which duly took place in January 1935 when 90.7 per cent voted to rejoin Germany. It was a small but satisfying victory for Hitler, who then claimed that Germany 'had no further territorial demands to make on France'.

The Spanish Civil War:
'Germany's destiny for good or bad'

In July 1936 Spain erupted in a bitter civil war that was to last until 1939, a war between fascism and democracy. With the Soviet Union lending her support to the left, both Italy and Germany lent their support, financially, morally and with military intervention, to General Francisco Franco's nationalist cause. The Spanish Civil War suited Hitler – it diverted international attention away from Germany while he steadily increased military output and gave his air force, still very new, the chance to test its wings in combat, most notoriously in April 1937 when the Luftwaffe bombed the Basque town of Guernica.

The civil war also brought about, in October 1936, the alliance of Germany and Italy and the signing of the Rome–Berlin Axis Pact. The following month, Germany signed the Anti-Comintern Pact with Japan, a mutual declaration against communist expansion, to which Mussolini added his signature a year later.

There were those in the higher echelons of the Nazi hierarchy who felt sufficiently worried about Hitler's expansionist plans to voice their concerns, including the army chief, Werner von Blomberg, who had done so much to help Hitler consolidate his power. In 1938, in a purge of his party, Hitler removed Blomberg and other moderates from power and replaced them with those more in tune with his own objectives. Abolishing the job of minister of war, Hitler appointed himself as commander-in-chief of the armed forces. One of those removed, the army commander-in-chief, Werner von Fritsch, later wrote: 'This man, Hitler, is Germany's destiny for good or bad. If he now goes over the abyss, he will drag us all down with him. There is nothing we can do.'

Anschluss: 'I can strongly recommend the Gestapo to one and all'

Following the First World War, the German-speaking Austrians desired unification, or *Anschluss*, with Germany, but it was forbidden under the Treaty of Versailles. As early as 1932, the Austrian Nazis won 16 per cent of the votes in a nationwide election.

In July 1934, the Austrian Nazis attempted an overthrow of the government, killing the chancellor, Engelbert Dollfuss, in the process but ultimately failing when the Austrian army stayed loyal to the government. Mussolini, a friend of Dollfuss, happened to be entertaining the chancellor's wife and children on the day of the assassination, and had to break the news to them. Outraged at the death of his friend, Mussolini pledged his support to the new chancellor, Kurt von Schuschnigg; and placed an army on the Austrian–Italian border at the Brenner Pass, ready to intervene at a moment's notice should the Nazis try again. Later, as Mussolini's allegiance moved towards Germany, this support was quietly withdrawn.

In 1938 Schuschnigg, fearing a renewed attack, demanded an audience with his fellow Austrian, Hitler. When Hitler did finally agree to meet the Austrian chancellor, he harangued him over the rights and the 'intolerable conditions' of the German-speaking Austrians and forced Schuschnigg into accepting a number of concessions, among them the inclusion of two Nazis in the Austrian government, most prominently Arthur Seyss-Inquart.

Browbeaten, Schuschnigg returned to Austria and decided to call for a referendum on whether his countrymen wanted independence or to be incorporated into the German Reich. Furious at Schuschnigg's audacity, Hitler demanded the cancellation of the referendum. Schuschnigg turned to Britain and France for help. When these leading representatives of the League of Nations were unable to assist, Schuschnigg bowed to the inevitable and resigned.

The new Austrian chancellor, the Nazi Seyss-Inquart, promptly invited the Germans into Austria to 'restore order'. On 12 March 1938, Hitler's troops marched into the city of Linz, followed a few hours later by Hitler himself, who received a rapturous welcome in his home town. On the following day, as Hitler paraded victoriously through the streets of Vienna, crowds cheered and shouted, 'Down with the Jews.' That same day the *Anschluss* was formally announced: Germany and Austria were as one.

Immediately the arrest and persecution of Austrian Jews began. Forced out of their homes, their businesses closed and liberties curtailed, the Jews were taunted and subjected to humiliation: the cleaning of pavements with toothbrushes or the hacking off of beards.

A referendum, held on 10 April, ratified the union; 99.5 per cent voted 'yes', although by this stage casting a 'no' vote would have been dangerous.

The 82-year-old Sigmund Freud, crippled by cancer, chose this moment to leave his homeland. Before departing for London, he was forced to write a complimentary reference about his treatment at the hands of the Nazis. He obliged, writing, 'I can strongly recommend the Gestapo to one and all.'

The Sudetenland: 'The last major problem to be solved'

The nation of Czechoslovakia was created in 1918 and among its diverse ethnic groups were the 3.5 million Germans living on the Czech–German border, in the Sudetenland. This was an area of 11,000 square miles and its German population, represented by the Nazi, Konrad Heinlein, demanded to be incorporated into the German Reich. Following the Austrian *Anschluss*, and encouraged by Hitler, their demands became more vocal. As Heinlein said, 'We must always demand so much that we can never be satisfied.' When the Czechoslovakian president, Eduard Benes, visited Hitler in Germany he was subjected to one of Hitler's harangues about oppression and the Sudeten Germans' right to self-determination. Hitler wanted to use the Sudetenland as a pretext to invade Czechoslovakia but his generals cautioned him against the idea.

On 15 September 1938, Neville Chamberlain, Britain's prime minister since May 1937, visited Hitler at his home in Berchtesgaden.

Hitler told Chamberlain that Czechoslovakia was the 'last major problem to be solved' and, despite his generals' advice and nervousness, threatened war unless the Czech and British governments accepted his demands that the Sudetenland be peacefully incorporated into the Reich. Chamberlain was not unsympathetic. Like many British politicians before him, he felt that Germany's treatment at Versailles had been unnecessarily unjust and the French determination to impose it to the letter overly harsh. Furthermore, a strong Germany, the British felt, would act as a useful buffer against the Soviet Union. Therefore, Chamberlain listened to Hitler and purposefully pursued a policy of appeasement.

When Chamberlain relayed Hitler's demands to Benes, the Czechoslovakian president knew he had no choice. Neither Britain nor France would come to his rescue, despite their alliances, and his country could not face going to war single-handedly against the might of Germany. Reluctantly, Benes agreed to Hitler's demands.

Chamberlain returned to Hitler, satisfied that, through his diplomacy, he had averted a war. But Hitler was now demanding more, namely the right to the immediate occupation of the Sudetenland and that the rights of Poland and Hungary, which each had territorial claims in Czechoslovakia, should also be recognized.

Chamberlain was prepared to accept these new demands but his government was not. A stalemate had been reached. Europe seemed on the brink of war until the unlikely figure of Mussolini stepped in as mediator and suggested a meeting between himself, Hitler, Chamberlain and the French prime minister, Édouard Daladier. The Czechoslovakian government was not invited.

The four powers met for one day in Munich on 29 September 1938. Germany, it was agreed, could have the Sudetenland in return for a guarantee that Hitler would make no further territorial demands – which would secure the rest of Czechoslovakia. Hitler agreed. But it left Czechoslovakia vulnerable – she had lost the natural defences of the Sudetenland that had acted as a buffer against Germany and had surrendered tracts of land to Poland and Hungary. Hitler and Chamberlain also signed a declaration of Anglo-German friendship, as 'symbolic of the desire of our two peoples never to go to war with one another again'.

Czechoslovakia: 'That senile old rascal'

Benes protested but was firmly reminded that no one would go to war over Czechoslovakia. The triumphant Chamberlain, meanwhile, returned to Britain, waving the infamous piece of paper in his hand, declaring that the Munich Agreement had guaranteed 'peace for our time'. Two days after the conference, on 1 October, the German army marched into the Sudetenland. Hitler, however, was far from satisfied with the outcome of Munich: 'That senile old rascal Chamberlain,' he complained, 'has ruined my entry into Prague.'

In the immediate aftermath of Munich, Hungary, Yugoslavia and Romania fell over themselves to sign various treaties and trade agreements with Germany. Poland, however, did not. Hitler wanted the return of Danzig which, as part of the Treaty of Versailles, had become part of Poland. But Poland held her ground and refused.

Over five months after occupying the Sudetenland, Hitler still considered the rest of Czechoslovakia as unfinished business. On 15 March 1939, he threatened and bullied the new Czechoslovakian president, Emil Hácha, until Hácha was forced to declare that he would 'confidently place the fate of the Czech people and country in the hands of the Führer and of the German Reich'. That same day, Hitler and his army marched into Prague to 'restore order'. Hitler was driven through the streets of the capital past rows of silent and glum spectators. Unlike Austria, there were no cheering crowds, no waving of flags. Britain and France failed to honour the agreement made at Munich nearly six months before, refusing to be drawn in, stating that Hácha had effectively invited Hitler in.

Up to the invasion of Czechoslovakia the British and French governments were able to persuade themselves that Hitler had only acted on behalf of German speakers – the Rhineland, Saar, in Austria and the Sudetenland. After March 1939, however, they could no longer hide behind this falsehood – Hitler had no right to invade Czechoslovakia. Appeasement was dead and Hitler was not a man to be trusted.

Poland – Guaranteed

The Treaty of Versailles had cut the German province of East Prussia off from the rest of Germany by a strip of land known as the Polish Corridor. At the end of this corridor, on the Baltic coast, was the former German port of Danzig, now declared a 'free city'. Germany demanded the return of Danzig and the construction of road and rail links through the Polish Corridor. The Polish government refused. The British and French governments, realizing Poland's vulnerability, offered Poland the guarantee that, if attacked, they would come to her aid. But in reality, neither Britain nor France had the military means to honour such a guarantee.

In May 1939, Hitler and Mussolini strengthened their ties by signing the 'Pact of Steel', a ten-year alliance. Chamberlain, despite being an ardent opponent of communism, saw the need to bring the Soviet Union into Britain's orbit if his guarantee to Poland was realistically to be upheld. But negotiations between the two nations failed – much to the delight of Hitler.

Between May and September 1939, the Soviet Union, engaged in a conflict in the east with Japan, had no desire to be pulled into a war against Germany on her western front. Germany too wanted to avoid a war against the Soviet Union and being forced into a war on two fronts. Hitler knew too that, despite the Pact of Steel, Italy was militarily weak and not ready for war.

Joseph Stalin realized that Hitler's ultimate territorial ambition was to invade the east. Hitler had never made a secret of this. But with the Soviet Union's military severely under strength, expediency overrode ideology and, on 23 August 1939, Germany and the Soviet Union amazed the world by signing a non-aggression pact. The pact committed the two nations to ten years of peace, together with a number of trade arrangements and, as a secret clause, the agreement to carve up various territories between them, including an east–west division of Poland. Hitler was delighted with the result and, on hearing the news, slapped his knee in characteristic joy. Without the aid of the Soviet Union, Hitler could not envisage Britain or France being capable of upholding their guarantee to the Poles. The road to Poland was now open.

Germany's War 1939: 'This country is at war with Germany'

On the evening of 31 August 1939, Himmler orchestrated a fake attack on the radio station in the German town of Gleiwitz on the German–Polish border. The 'attacked Germans' had, in self-defence, shot dead some of the Polish assailants, and they produced the photographic evidence to prove it. But the dead Polish soldiers were in fact inmates from a German concentration camp. It may all have been an obvious lie but Hitler used it as his pretext for invasion.

At 4.45 on the morning of Friday, 1 September 1939, the whole weight of Germany's military might fell on Poland in a lightning attack (Blitzkrieg). Following up the rapid advances, German forces engaged in brutality, executions and merciless aggression against the civilian population.

Chamberlain, making good his guarantee of five months earlier, declared war on Germany on 3 September. In a broadcast speech, he announced: 'This morning the British ambassador in Berlin handed the German government a final note stating that, unless we heard from them by eleven o'clock that they were prepared at once to withdraw their troops from Poland, a state of war would exist between us. I have to tell you now that no such undertaking has been received, and that consequently this country is at war with Germany.'

Six hours later, the French dutifully followed suit and also declared war on Germany.

The British contribution to the Polish cause, however, was not with arms, nor soldiers nor aid, but with leaflets – by the million, dropped by plane over Germany, urging the population to stand up against the war.

On 17 September, as the German war machine advanced its way towards Warsaw, the Soviet Union, as secretly agreed in the Non-Aggression Pact, attacked from the east. Crushed between two totalitarian heavyweights, Poland crumbled, and on the twenty-seventh Warsaw surrendered. Agreeing on the partition of Poland, the Germans and Russians then set about the total subjugation of the defeated population: villages razed, inhabitants massacred, the Polish identity eradicated, and in towns such as Lodz, Jews herded into ghettos before eventual transportation to the death camps. Hitler visited Warsaw on 5 October and, casting a satisfied eye over the devastated capital, declared, 'this is how I deal with any European city'. With another of his objectives achieved, Hitler could have made overtures towards peace talks. No such suggestions were made.

Germany's War: 1940 to 1941

Hitler's Germany enjoyed a run of success during the early years of the Second World War. Having defeated Poland, on 9 April 1940 Hitler turned to the invasion of Scandinavia and there forced Denmark into surrender in only a matter of hours. On 10 June, Norway capitulated.

In 1940, the war turned to the Low Countries. Both Belgium and the Netherlands capitulated as the Germans swept through northern France, brushing aside the French army. The British army, sent as reinforcements, was pushed back to the port of Dunkirk and forced into a frantic evacuation back to Britain. France fell in June 1940. Only Britain remained to fight the Germans. Hitler planned to invade England but needed control of the skies above southern England as a prelude to a full-blown attack. However, the RAF kept the Luftwaffe at bay during the Battle of Britain and cities throughout the country survived the

Blitz to the point Hitler postponed his plans for invasion indefinitely.

In June 1940, Mussolini entered the war and attacked Greece and then Libya, but was soon forced into retreat. Hitler sent forces to aid the situation, conquering Greece, Crete and also Yugoslavia, and committing to a long struggle in North Africa. In June 1941, Hitler launched Operation Barbarossa – the invasion of the Soviet Union – less than two years after the signing of the Non-Aggression Pact and its agreement of ten years of peace. The German advance through Russia was spectacular. But with their lines of communication stretched the further they advanced, and with the weather turning against them, the German juggernaut ground to a halt only fifteen miles short of Moscow.

On 7 December 1941, the Japanese attacked Pearl Harbor, bringing the US into the war. Four days later, Hitler declared war on America. The war was now truly a global conflict.

Germany's War: 1942 to 1945

In 1942 British and Commonwealth forces defeated the Germans in North Africa at El Alamein. In the Soviet Union, in February 1943, the Germans surrendered at Stalingrad, following an abrasive and epic battle, in what is generally considered the turning point of the war. Five months later, the Germans lost the biggest tank battle of the war at Kursk. In May 1943, the Germans surrendered in North Africa.

After a sustained campaign in Italy, the Allies eventually reached Rome, defeating the Germans along the way. Italy deserted the Axis and swapped sides, joining forces with the Allies. Mussolini fled, to be later caught and summarily executed.

As the armies of the Soviet Union began to recapture the territory that had been won by the Germans, the Allies launched the second front on 6 June 1944, landing in Normandy in occupied France. By August Paris had been liberated, followed nine days later by Brussels. In December 1944, Hitler launched the Battle of the Bulge, but this last-ditch offensive was pushed back as the Allies advanced through France and into Germany.

By April 1945, Berlin was surrounded by the Allies coming in from the west, and the Soviet armies from the east. The death camps were liberated, revealing to the world the full horror of the 'Final Solution' and Hitler's determination to rid Europe of Jews. On 28 April, Hitler married his long-term girlfriend, Eva Braun, and two days later the couple committed suicide. A week later, on 7 May, Germany surrendered unconditionally.

The war in Europe had ended. Three months later, following the dropping of atomic bombs in Hiroshima and Nagasaki, Japan also surrendered.

The Second World War, which had lasted 2,192 days, was over, and with it, after twelve years, the Nazi dream of the thousand-year Third Reich.

Appendix One: Key Players

Adolf Hitler 1889–1945

In January 1945, with the Soviet Red Army bearing down on Germany, Hitler left his HQ in East Prussia and moved back to Berlin and into the Reich Chancellery. In April, he moved underground into the Chancellery's air-raid shelter, a cavern of dimly lit rooms made of thick, high-quality concrete.

Hitler's health during his last few months deteriorated rapidly. In February he had to have an operation on his vocal cords as a result of so many years of shouting. Following the operation he was obliged to remain silent for a whole week.

Hitler refused to leave Berlin, and when he realized the war was truly lost, he decided to end his life.

Hitler looked much older than his fifty-six years – he shuffled around with a stoop, his left hand shook continuously, perhaps from the onset of Parkinson's Disease, and he had to have daily doses of cocaine drops in his right eye to quell a new pain. He had fallen out with many of his senior colleagues – in particular Göring and Himmler. Goebbels, however, remained loyal to the last.

On 20 April, Hitler's fifty-sixth and final birthday, a group of twenty Hitler Youth boys were lined up in the Chancellery for Hitler to inspect. In single file from the eldest to the youngest, Hitler, with his shaking left hand behind his back, shook hands with each child, pinching the cheek of the last, the youngest child. He delivered a brief speech and thanked them for their bravery before shuffling back into the bunker. It was to be Hitler's last public appearance.

On 28 April, in a ten-minute ceremony, Hitler married Eva Braun. She was twenty-three years his junior, and the German public knew nothing of her. Her presence, although not a secret among the Nazi hierarchy, was not something Hitler wanted publicized lest it should diminish the adoration of Germany's women for the Führer.

That evening Hitler dictated his will to his secretary, in which he drew up the composition of the government following his death. The admiral, Karl Donitz, was named as his successor, not as Führer but as president.

On 29 April, with the Soviets barely 300 metres away, Hitler made preparations for his death. Benzene was brought in. Hitler insisted that his body be burnt after his death. He did not want his corpse to end up in Soviet hands, like an 'exhibit in a cabinet of curiosities'. He ordered the testing of the newly arrived batch of cyanide capsules and the chosen victim was Hitler's beloved Alsatian dog, Blondi.

On 30 April, Goebbels tried one last time to persuade the Führer to leave Berlin.

At just before four o'clock, after a series of farewells, Hitler and his wife of forty-eight hours retired to his study. Hitler wore upon his tunic his Iron Cross (First Class) and his Wounded badge from the First World War. A shot was heard.

Hitler had shot himself through the right temple. Braun was also dead. She had taken the cyanide.

The bodies, covered in blankets, were carried out into the Chancellery garden. There, with artillery exploding around them and neighbouring buildings ablaze, Hitler's wishes were honoured – 200 litres of benzene were poured over the corpses and they were set alight.

Ernst Röhm 1887–1934

An army captain from the First World War, Röhm joined the Freikorps and helped the Weimar Republic keep order during the turbulent post-war years.

He met Hitler during the early days of the Nazi Party, resigned from the army and was appointed by Hitler as chief of the SA.

However, after Hitler's appointment as chancellor in 1933, Röhm felt that Hitler had gone soft and had not given the SA its due reward for helping the Nazis into power. The SA started talking of a 'second revolution' with Röhm as the leader of a People's Party, talk that greatly alarmed the industrialists and businessmen whom Hitler had managed to woo. Röhm wanted also to merge the army with the SA under his command, which, in turn, alarmed the army.

The SA's violence, which once, as a revolutionary, Hitler would have endorsed, had become an embarrassment. The SA's agitation was beginning to damage the country's stability, and President Hindenburg threatened to bring in martial law unless Hitler could bring the situation under control.

On the weekend of 30 June–1 July 1934, in what was to become known as the 'Night of the Long Knives', Hitler acted. Members of the SS stormed a hotel in the village of Bad Wiessee where the SA had gathered for a weekend of debauchery, pulled Röhm and his henchmen from their beds and had them arrested. They were all promptly executed, including Röhm who, having passed up the opportunity to take his own life, was shot.

Paul von Hindenburg 1847–1934

Hindenburg had fought in the Franco-Prussian War of 1870–71 and had retired as commander of the German armed forces in 1911.

He was called back to office in 1914 and was instrumental in Germany's success on the Eastern Front during the First World War.

In 1925 he was elected president of the Weimar Republic and re-elected in 1932, defeating the Nazi Party. Despite the growing popularity of the Nazis, Hindenburg initially resisted calls to invite Hitler into his coalition government. However, persuaded by Franz von Papen, he relented and Hitler was appointed chancellor in January 1933. Increasingly senile, Hindenburg took little active part in the affairs of state.

Following the Reichstag Fire a month after Hitler's appointment, Hindenburg allowed his chancellor to temporarily suspend the constitution until the threat to the country was eliminated (a measure that was never revoked).

Hindenburg died, aged eighty-six, in August 1934.

Joseph Goebbels 1897–1945

Having initially flirted with communism, Goebbels became a firm Nazi and a devotee of Hitler. Small in stature and impaired by a club foot, he was a man of great if warped intellect, as shown in his diaries. In 1921, he gained a doctorate in philosophy.

On coming to power, Hitler appointed Goebbels his propaganda minister, a role at which Goebbels excelled, controlling all forms of German media.

As the war turned against Germany, Goebbels' devotion remained undiminished and in his broadcasts to the nation he urged the German population to show greater commitment to the cause.

Not wanting his children to live in a post-Nazi society, on the day following Hitler's suicide, Goebbels and his wife, Magda, poisoned their six children before taking their own lives.

Heinrich Himmler 1900–45

With his rimless glasses and small physique, Himmler's appearance was at odds with his fearsome manner. After a stint in the army during the First World War, Himmler became a chicken farmer before joining the Nazis and taking part in the failed Munich Putsch of 1923. Hitler appointed him head of the SS and, in 1934, head of all Nazi security forces, including the Gestapo. Himmler played a vital role in the elimination of Hitler's opponents during the 'Night of the Long Knives'.

During the war he was responsible for coordinating the systematic murder of Jews and other victims of the Nazi regime. But as the war turned against Germany, Himmler sought peace negotiations with the Western allies in order to carry on the fight against the Soviet Union. Labelled a traitor by Hitler, he was stripped of all his responsibilities.

After Germany's surrender, Himmler tried to escape detention, dressing up as a policeman. But caught by the British, Himmler committed suicide by poison before he could be brought to trial.

Hermann Göring 1893–1946

A dashing fighter pilot during the First World War, Göring joined the Nazi Party in 1922 and a year later was injured during the failed Munich Putsch, after which he escaped for four years to Austria.

Göring helped Hitler in destroying the SA during the 'Night of the Long Knives' and in 1935 was appointed commander-in-chief of the Luftwaffe. The following year he was also appointed economics minister. Göring's grasp of economics was questionable but, with Hitler's prompting, he introduced the Four-Year Plan, an aggressive policy to prepare Germany for war.

Göring's power fluctuated in line with the successes and failures of the Luftwaffe. After initial successes during the Polish and French campaigns in the first year of the Second World War, reverses during the Battle of Britain and Stalingrad, and the Luftwaffe's failure to prevent the bombing of German cities, saw the decline of Göring's influence.

Göring was tried at Nuremberg and sentenced to be hanged. His plea for death by firing squad, a 'soldier's death', was refused and two hours before his execution he took his own life using poison that had been smuggled in to him.

Franz von Papen 1879–1969

Von Papen was appointed chancellor by President Hindenburg in 1932. However, in the elections of July that year, Papen's authority was diminished by the success of the Nazi Party which polled almost 40 per cent of the vote. He offered Hitler a post within his cabinet which the Nazi leader turned down.

A second election, in November 1932, signalled the end for von Papen as he lost his post as chancellor. But his replacement, Schleicher, also failed to command a majority with the Reichstag, so von Papen, intrigued by Hitler, suggesting Hitler become chancellor, with von Papen his vice-chancellor.

Von Papen took his proposal to Hindenburg, arguing it would be easier to contain Hitler inside the government rather than have him agitating from the outside. The power, von Papen maintained, would lie with himself. Hindenburg initially resisted but then changed his mind and in January 1933 Hitler was duly appointed chancellor, with von Papen at his side.

But von Papen's scheme backfired and, unable to contain Hitler, he made a speech in June 1934 criticizing the SA's violent methods.

Fortunate to escape with his life during the 'Night of the Long Knives', von Papen resigned as vice-chancellor and took up an appointment as German ambassador in Austria where he played a role in the *Anschluss*.

Tried at Nuremberg, von Papen was sentenced to eight years' imprisonment but was released after two.

Benito Mussolini 1883–1945

Mussolini worked as a schoolteacher and journalist and was wounded during the First World War. Having been a socialist, after the war Mussolini formed the Fascist Party.

In 1922, with Italy on the brink of civil war between the far-right and communist groups, Mussolini demanded the installation of a fascist government. The Italian king, Victor Emmanuel III, wanting to avoid a conflict, invited Mussolini to Rome to form a government, an event known as the 'March on Rome'.

The Fascist Party won the election of 1924, and within two years Mussolini was ruling as dictator, or Duce, suppressing all opposition and dissent.

Initially, Mussolini opposed Germany's Nazism, especially Hitler's claim on Austria. Mussolini was friends with the Austrian leader, Engelbert Dollfuss, and following Dollfuss's assassination in 1934, Mussolini pledged his support to Austria.

However, after international condemnation of Italy's invasion of Abyssinia, Mussolini sided with Hitler and in 1936 the two nations formed the Axis.

After an initial delay, Italy joined the war in June 1940, but her campaigns in Greece and North Africa were disastrous and needed Germany's intervention.

By July 1943, the Allies had invaded Italy, and unable to maintain support, Mussolini was summoned by the king, dismissed, arrested and imprisoned as Italy swapped sides and joined the Allies.

In mid-September, on Hitler's orders, Mussolini was sprung from his captivity, taken to Germany, and returned to Italy as the puppet head of a fascist republic in German-occupied northern Italy.

With the end in sight, Mussolini, his mistress, Clara Petacci, and a few followers attempted to escape into Switzerland but they were stopped by Italian partisans. Mussolini's attempts to disguise himself with a Luftwaffe overcoat and helmet had failed, and on 28 April 1945, at Lake Como, Mussolini and Petacci were shot. Their bodies were transported to Milan where they were beaten and urinated upon and finally left to hang upside down for public display.

Neville Chamberlain 1869–1940

Before the Second World War, Chamberlain served as the Conservative minister of health and chancellor of the exchequer. In May 1937, the prime minister, Stanley Baldwin, resigned and Chamberlain took his place.

His time as prime minister was dominated by foreign affairs, namely Britain's dealings with Germany. Pursuing a policy of appeasement, Chamberlain believed in assuaging Hitler's grievances, which he felt were, in the main, justified. Having negotiated an end to the Czechoslovakian crisis in 1938, he returned to Britain convinced that Hitler, as an honourable man, had been satisfied. Between them, Chamberlain and Hitler had secured 'peace for our time'.

The next crisis, over Poland, illustrated Chamberlain's folly in believing appeasement could contain Hitler, and Chamberlain was quick to offer a guarantee to Poland.

Chamberlain kept his word and, when Germany invaded Poland in September 1939, Britain declared war on Germany.

The government's handling of the Norwegian campaign was heavily criticized, and following the capitulation of Norway and Denmark, Chamberlain, unable to form a coalition government, was forced to resign. His successor, in May 1940, was Winston Churchill.

Already ill, Chamberlain was dead within six months.

Appendix Two:
Timeline of Nazi Germany

1918

October: Start of the 'German Revolution'.

9 November: The German Kaiser, Wilhelm II, abdicates.

9 November: Friedrich Ebert proclaims Germany a republic.

11 November: Germany's defeat and the end of the First World War.

1919

5 –12 January: Spartacists, German communists, stage an uprising in Berlin.

19 January: First German democratic elections.

11 August: Weimar Republic constitution ratified.

28 June: Treaty of Versailles signed in the Hall of Mirrors.

12 September: Hitler attends a meeting of DAP, the German Workers' Party.

1920

24 February: DAP becomes the Nationalist Socialist German Workers' Party, or NSDAP.

13 March: The Kapp Putsch fails in Berlin.

1921

29 July: Hitler becomes leader of NSDAP.

1923

11 January: French and Belgian forces occupy the Ruhr.

8 November: The Munich Putsch, led by Hitler, fails.

1924

1 April: Hitler is sentenced to five years but serves less than nine months.

1925

18 July: First of two volumes of Hitler's autobiography, *Mein Kampf*, is published.

July: French and Belgian forces withdraw from the Ruhr.

1926

8 September: Germany joins the League of Nations.

1932

31 July: Reichstag elections – the Nazis poll almost 40 per cent of the vote.

1933

30 January: Hitler appointed chancellor within a coalition government.

27 February: The Reichstag Fire.

20 March: Dachau, the first concentration camp, is opened.

23 March: Passing of the Enabling Act.

26 April: The Gestapo, the Nazi secret police, is formed.

10 May: 25,000 'un-German' books burnt across Germany.

14 October: Germany withdraws from the League of Nations.

1934

30 June–1 July: 'Night of the Long Knives'.

2 August: President Hindenburg dies.

1935

13 January: Saar plebiscite – 90.7 per cent vote to rejoin Germany.
15 September: Nuremberg Race Laws come into effect.

1936

7 March: German army enters the Rhineland.
17 July: Start of the Spanish Civil War.
1 August: Start of the Berlin Olympics.
25 October: Signing of the Rome–Berlin Axis.
25 November: Germany and Japan sign the Anti-Comintern Pact.

1937

26 April: The Luftwaffe bomb the Basque town of Guernica.
6 November: Italy joins Germany and Japan in the Anti-Comintern Pact.

1938

4 February: Hitler appoints himself commander-in-chief of the armed forces.
12 March: German army enters Austria and *Anschluss* is declared the following day.
29 September: Munich Agreement signed.
1 October: German army occupies the Sudetenland.
9 November: Kristallnacht or the 'Night of Broken Glass'.

1939

15 March: German invasion of Czechoslovakia.
22 May: Germany and Italy sign the 'Pact of Steel'.
23 August: Germany and Soviet Union sign the Non-Aggression Pact.
1 September: Germany invades Poland – start of Second World War.

3 September: Britain and France declare war on Germany.
27 September: Surrender of Warsaw.

1940

9 April: Germany invades Denmark and Norway.
10 May: Germany invades Belgium, Holland and Luxembourg.
15 May: Holland surrenders to Germany.
28 May: Belgium surrenders to Germany.
10 June: Capitulation of Norway.
22 June: France signs armistice with Germany.
13 August: Battle of Britain begins.

1941

30 March: German Afrika Korps begin offensive in North Africa.
6 April: Germany invades Yugoslavia and Greece.
17 April: Yugoslav army surrenders to Germany.
22 June: Operation Barbarossa – Germany invades Soviet Union.
11 December: Germany declares war on US.

1942

23 August: Stalingrad offensive begins.
23 October: Second Battle of El Alamein begins.

1943

2 February: German surrender at Stalingrad.
13 May: Axis forces in North Africa surrender.
13 October: Italy declares war on Germany.

1944

6 June: Operation Overlord – Allied invasion of Normandy.
20 July: Attempted assassination of Hitler.
25 August: Allies liberate Paris.

3 September: Allies liberate Brussels.

23 October: Soviets enter East Prussia.

4 November: Surrender of Axis forces in Greece.

1945

27 January: Soviets liberate Auschwitz.

23 April: Soviets enter Berlin.

30 April: Hitler commits suicide.

7 May: German unconditional surrender to the Allies and Soviet Union.

Got Another Hour?

History in an Hour is a series of eBooks to help the reader learn the basic facts of a given subject area. Everything you need to know is presented in a straightforward narrative and in chronological order. No embedded links to divert your attention, nor a daunting book of 600 pages with a 35-page introduction. Just straight in, to the point, sixty minutes, done. Then, having absorbed the basics, you may feel inspired to explore further. Give yourself sixty minutes and see what you can learn…

To find out more visit http://historyinanhour.com or follow us on twitter: http://twitter.com/historyinanhour

1066: History in an Hour by Kaye Jones

Covering the major events of the year 1066, this is a clear account of England's political turmoil during which the country had three different kings and fought three large-scale battles in defence of the kingdom, including the infamous Battle of Hastings.

The Afghan Wars: History in an Hour by Rupert Colley

A comprehensive overview of the wars that have been fought in Afghanistan for almost four decades, including the politics of the Taliban, why Osama Bin Laden was so significant, and why it is still so hard to achieve peace in the country.

The American Civil War: History in an Hour by Kat Smutz

A clear account of the politics and major turning points of the war that split the country in half as the northern and southern states fought over the right to keep slaves, changing American culture forever.

American Slavery: History in an Hour by Kat Smutz

A broad overview of the major events in the history of American slavery, detailing the arrival of the first slaves, the Southern plantations, the Civil War, and the historical and cultural legacy of slavery in the United States.

Ancient Egypt: History in an Hour by Anthony Holmes

A succinct exploration of the historic rise of Egyptian civilisation and its influence on the world, covering Egyptian gods, mummification and burial rituals, and the Pyramids of Giza.

Black History: History in an Hour by Rupert Colley

A clear overview of the long and varied history of African Americans, including everything from slavery, the Civil War and emancipation to the civil rights movement and the Black Panther Party.

The Cold War: History in an Hour by Rupert Colley

A succinct overview of the politics of the non-violent war, from the end of World War II to the collapse of the USSR in 1991, as Russia and America eyed each other with suspicion and hostility.

Dickens: History in an Hour by Kaye Jones

A comprehensive overview of the life of arguably Britain's most successful and beloved writer, including the poverty of his childhood, the evolution of his novels, his tours of Europe and America, and his occasionally scandalous private life.

George Washington: History in an Hour by David B. McCoy

The essential chronicle of George Washington's life, from his middle-class Virginian upbringing to his unanimous election as America's first president, and the prominent role he played in shaping America as we know it today.

The Gunpowder Plot: History in an Hour by Sinead Fitzgibbon

An engaging account of the infamous plot by a group of Catholic traitors, led by Guy Fawkes, to blow up the Houses of Parliament and James I, including details of the motives behind their drastic actions and how the plot came to be discovered.

Henry VIII's Wives: History in an Hour by Julie Wheeler

An inclusive introduction to the six diverse personalities of Henry VIII's wives, the events that led them to their individual fates, and the different impacts they each had on King and country.

Hitler: History in an Hour by Rupert Colley

A coherent overview of Hitler's early life, service in World War I, rise to the top of the Nazi Party and eventually the head of state, covering all the key moments of the dictator's life through to his death and the crumbling of his empire.

JFK: History in an Hour by Sinead Fitzgibbon

A comprehensive insight into the life of America's youngest elected president, assassinated barely one thousand days into his presidency, examining his navigation of the Space Race, his sympathies with the civil rights movement, and the chronic illness that affected him throughout his life.

The Medieval Anarchy: History in an Hour by Kaye Jones

A look at the unprecedented chaos and disorder that followed the death of King Henry I, leading to England's first, and often forgotten, civil war, as well as an overview of the plots and violence that ensued during this nineteen-year bloody conflict.

The Queen: History in an Hour by Sinead Fitzgibbon

A compelling history of the UK's second-longest-reigning monarch, covering her 1953 coronation to her Diamond Jubilee in 2012 and examining her long reign, during which the British Empire has transformed.

The Reformation: History in an Hour by Edward A. Gosselin

A concise look at the spread of religious dissidence across Europe in the sixteenth century, including the events that caused people to question the ideas of the established Catholic Church and the resulting wars, migration and disunity.

The Russian Revolution: History in an Hour by Rupert Colley

Covering all the major events in a straightforward overview of the greatest political experiment ever conducted, and how it continues to influence both Eastern and Western politics today.

The Siege of Leningrad: History in an Hour by Rupert Colley

A broad account of one of the longest sieges in history in which over the course of 900 days the city of Leningrad resisted German invasion, contributing to the defeat of the Nazis at the cost of over one million civilian lives.

South Africa: History in an Hour by Anthony Holmes

A fascinating overview of South Africa's history of oppression and racial inequality and how after years of violence and apartheid, Nelson Mandela, the country's first black President, led the country to unite and become the 'Rainbow Nation'.

Stalin: History in an Hour by Rupert Colley

A succinct exploration of Joseph Stalin's long leadership of the Soviet Union, covering his rise to power, his role in the Russian Revolution, and his terrifying regime that directly and negatively affected the lives of so many.

Titanic: History in an Hour by Sinead Fitzgibbon

An account of the catastrophe, including the failures of the White Star Line, the significance of class and the legacy of the disaster in Britain and America.

The Vietnam War: History in an Hour by Neil Smith

A clear account of the key events of the most important Cold War-era conflict, including the circumstances leading up to the Vietnam War, the deadly guerrilla warfare, the fall of Saigon and the backlash of anti-war protests in America.

World War One: History in an Hour by Rupert Colley

A clear overview of the road to war, the major turning points and battles, and the key leaders involved, as well as the lasting impact the Great War had on almost every country in the world.

World War Two: History in an Hour by Rupert Colley

Covering the major events in a broad overview of the politics and violence of the most devastating conflict the world has ever seen, and how it changed the world in unimaginable ways.